The Long Hot Summer
2022

haiku & photographs

Judith Lauter

To order additional copies of this book, contact:
Xlibris
844-714-8691
www.Xlibris.com
Orders@Xlibris.com

Photo credits: Cover and most interior photographs by the author; velvet-ant photo on p. 30, taken by Mark Musselman, USFWS, is public domain, downloaded from PIXNIO, under a Free-to-Use Creative Commons license; back-cover photo by Ken Lauter, used with permission.

ISBN: Softcover   978-1-6698-4974-2
       EBook   978-1-6698-4973-5

Print information available on the last page

Rev. date: 09/29/2022

* * *

to Ken

who watched all these goings-on with me
in amazement –
'like nothing we'd ever seen before'

CONTENTS

Preface: Pictures, Poems, & Meteorology

On Wednesday, January 6, 2021, my husband Ken and I were sitting in a rental condo on North Padre Island off the Texas Gulf Coast, just back from a walk on the beach – mid-60s, coastal clouds, breezy. We had spent a month there, celebrating our 20th year in Texas – for me a return to my home state after many years away. When we turned on the TV, we were startled to see a chaotic crowd of ragamuffins clambering up the walls of the Capitol in DC. Staring in disbelief, I said, 'Who *are* those bozos? What *do* they think they're doing?' The answers were not long in coming.

Three days later we made the eight-hour drive north to our home in Nacogdoches, and the next morning, as we returned from a lunch of Mexican food, we saw a light snow beginning to fall. Ken and I had spent our early years in the Midwest (Michigan for me, Missouri for him), and after many endless winters smothered in snow and what I called 'black cold,' we were glad to re-locate to the 'pineywoods' of East Texas, where winters are green and warm, and snow rare.

So a modest Texas-style snowfall was pleasant, an unusual January diversion. The snow continued into the evening; we could see it beginning to build up in the flourishing grass of our yard. Around 8 pm, again watching TV, we heard a thunderous bang on the roof – and discovered a ragged, four-foot-long pine branch thrust through the ceiling above our bed. Snow was filtering down around the branch.

That began a strange odyssey, as extreme winter weather collided with political mismanagement. The next morning, instead of waking to mainly a wet yard, with the snow melted, as expected, we found we were snowed in – snow six inches deep covering the yard and driveway, massive tree branches broken and tumbled into ice-covered piles, our azalea bushes bowed over with the weight of snow and ice.

No city services turned up to clear the street. (Nacogdoches has no city snow-plows; Dallas bought their first ones in 2011.) City streets and local highways were snow-covered, stores were closed, parking lots empty. City water went out – another group of bozos, who control the electric grid in Texas, had instituted rolling blackouts that shut down the water plant, so we had no water for five days. (Our own house power stayed intact, thanks to a Generac we bought in 2018.) Hoarders cleaned out the few stores that did open, so bottled water could not be found. We had to melt snow and ice for the toilets, and boil it for drinking.

Somehow we got through the week and thought the trouble was over. Then five weeks later, the infamous storm of 2021 (Winter Storm Uri, or as the papers called it, the Valentine-Week Winter Storm) hit the state between Feb. 13 and 17 – knocking out power and water across a much larger region, killing 246 people across Texas, 43 in Houston alone, more than half of them dying from hypothermia – they froze to death. (A year later, the same bozo-club is still in charge of the Texas power grid.)

The spring that tried to arrive that year was a terrible thing to see. In usually abundantly-green East Texas, so many plants had been stressed by the ice and cold that some could not manage to put out even a few leaves. Nacogdoches is known for its azaleas – but in the spring of 2021 few bloomed, and those that did were puny, a single flower here and there. Many trees, both in towns and along country roads, produced a few leaves down near the trunk, but their upper branches remained bare, dying if not dead. People not only cut back the dead branches of trees in their yards, to protect against their falling on houses, but also had whole trees taken out, with an eye to creating what they call in the Mountain West 'defensible space,' a clear area around a house where, in this case, falling branches, or a whole tree that succumbed, could not threaten the house. (See Endnotes for more on 'defensible space.')

* * *

Even now, more than a year later, many trees in East Texas still display a halo of dead upper branches, a ghostly reminder of the devastating snow and cold. But this spring, it looked like things were coming back – the familiar green of the pine forest began to re-assert itself in astounding fullness and beauty. Most trees were bursting with leaves, flowering bushes did their thing, the azaleas were back!

I'm fond of flowers, and since coming to Nacogdoches, have taken the opportunity of the year-round growing season to put in more plants around our house than the places we'd lived before – Arizona, Colorado, Missouri, Oklahoma. With the green returning, I tried some new approaches to decorating our flower beds – featuring a rainbow-colored series of tall snapdragons, bordered by river rocks. I had great hopes of watching my experiments flourish throughout a kinder, gentler spring and summer.

But in mid-May (sixteen months after the 2021 ice storm), a series of international heat waves began that would last into September. Countries around the world felt the heat – several in Europe experienced record-high triple-digit temperatures leading to heat deaths and evacuations, with a record high of 116.6 degrees F reported in Portugal, along with droughts and wildfires. Similar conditions affected parts of the Middle East, North Africa, and across Asia. In mid-July it reached 126 degrees in Iran, Tunisia reported a 40-year high of 118 degrees, and in parts of China, where records have been kept since 1873, record highs in the 100s destroyed highways and roofs.

Texas had been suffering under drought conditions since the previous year, and things only got worse in summer 2022 as the heat went on rising (see the Endnotes for the poems *Weeks and weeks over 100*, and *Finally, rain*). Then in early September, a unique giant heat dome arrived that covered much of the Western U.S., bringing record daytime and night-time highs, combined with high humidity, to California, Arizona, and Nevada. Sixty million people were under heat warnings, advisories, and alerts.

The situation was finally relieved by a tropical storm that broke up the dome. Observers said this heat event would rank among the worst in four decades. Some meteorologists predicted that within the next decade, the summer of 2022 would become the norm around the world, and should be acknowledged as 'the coolest we will see for some time.'

As the spring and summer went on, the heat in Nacogdoches seemed worse and worse – and I was particularly alert to an outbreak of wildfires in the mountains of northern New Mexico, where for two decades we've been spending our second month-away each year, near Taos. Fires had broken out near some of our favorite towns, and the conflagrations, fanned by unseasonably strong winds, began spreading steadily northward toward the high green valley where we usually stayed. Every day I checked the 'Active Fires' and 'Fire Perimeters' options on the Weather Underground map to track the progress of the fires. A webcam in the valley showed that the air was sometimes orange, filled with smoke blowing up from the fires which crept to within 50 miles of the valley before the monsoons finally swept in and shut them down.

As I watched the mountain fires move northward across the online maps, followed the steady worsening of the international extreme weather along with the rise in our local temps, and worked to keep the heat from killing my flowers, it occurred to me that I ought to put together a collection of haiku and photos to record the experience of the brutal summer. (I chose my title not with any reference to the 1958 movie, but because I felt the phrase best suited what the book was about.)

* * *

I am devoted to the planet, and love to chronicle her moods and seasons, but the facts of this summer were virtually beyond poetry, something far bigger than the limited view available from our little town in East TX. And yet I hope that readers of this book will see it as a small song of celebration for the beauty of the Earth – if humans (who, let's face it, have become an invasive species to everything: the ground, the water, plants, and other animals) will just *leave it alone*.

So I offer the book as an apology to the Earth, a whispered prayer to her, that we humans can somehow come to our senses, that the 'long hot summers' and the 'long cold winters' will return to normal levels and allow the Earth to rebound as we, her children, know She can, as along with her we swing on the ancient elliptical path around our star, the sun that gives us life, that gives us everything.

The Long Hot Summer

2022

Preliminaries

Only 16 months ago

Grid broke, water-plant broke, pine
branches broke, hole in
the roof – snow too deep for Texas!

Promise of rebound, March 2022

We thought we were back, Queen Green
ruling the world, pinks
and plums where sapphire drifts were.

Fond hopes of spring

My first try at river rocks,
a forest of snap-
dragons – all dead by July.

The Summer

Long Hot Summer

Cicada shells left on the
bedroom screen, snails mark
the door. AC runs all night.

24

Weeks and weeks over 100

In low tones, dove mourns the loss
of normalcy: e-
ven mockingbirds don't sing now.

Gerbera maintenance schedule

I provide quilts in winter,
shade in summer, now
bright faces remind me why.

Pond at the bottom of our hill

Never goes dry. Deep spigot
of seawater, cleaned
through sand – freshwater on tap.

Photo by Mark Musselman, USFWS

Escape of the velvet ant
[or, why I didn't get my own photo]

Too hot for her, too – burnt red
by this eternal
sunshine, she's shade-bound and down.

Succulents are right at home

El patrón agave takes
on all comers, sharp-
edged teeth bite more than a lime.

Cattle egrets' roosting tree

Dim before dawn – but at night
(once all have come home)
a tree bright with white candles.

Designated look-outs

We watch over the hill for
the rest of the herd –
grasshoppers leaping like leaves.

*[a local egret flyway at sunrise; the birds were out-of-frame
before I could retrieve my camera]*

Impersonating roseates

High above, cattle egrets
off to their long day,
underwings pink with sunrise.

Reprieve

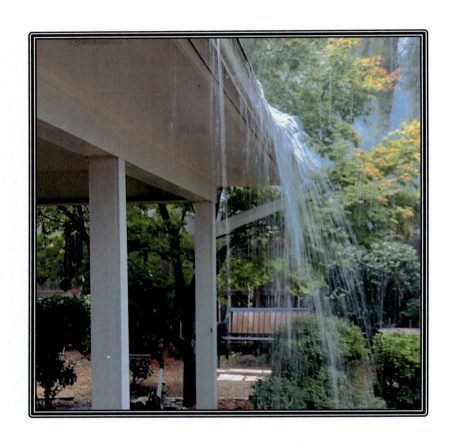

Finally, rain

Rivers fall from the sky straight
to our roof, cascades
leaving all gutters behind.

Puffball (?) mushroom

Finally grew a stalk (– not a
puffball!), raising its
'brella like us, glad for rain.

Fungi everywhere

Even a small rain calls them
from the dark, some gnarled,
others tender as petals.

Snail after rain

Traversing our kitchen screen,
she carries her house,
peering in at me, in mine.

September resurgence

Fat with surprising rain, chock-
ful of sap, making
leaves, making up a lost year.

Rainy sunset

Clouds upon clouds, promising
even more rain to
come – we'll all have green dreams now.

Deck-the-halls fall

Creepers celebrate, hanging
neighborhood fences
in Christmas-come-early red.

Endnotes

Cover image. The edge of a grassy yard in early morning, along a curb lined with trapezoidal concrete retaining-wall blocks. The rising sun is just high enough to throw a line of shadows of the upper edges of the stones down onto the pavement across the cream-colored gutter pan. The combination of organic-bright-green grass against the inorganic-stone-colors of blocks, gutter, shadows, and pavement – all in their own ways depending on sunshine for their part in the picture – seemed an appropriate symbol for the summer's dramatic duel between sun-as-physics (heat, light, shade), and sun-as-life-giver (helping grass grow).

Preface. 'Defensible space' was a concept promoted in the 1970s by the architect Oscar Newman, referring to ways of making residences crime-resistant in urban areas, but the growing threat of wildfires in the Western U.S. over the last two decades has resulted in the concept being re-purposed to refer to protecting homes from wildfires. As of 2021, California's Office of the State Fire Marshal began requiring that anyone selling real estate located in a state-defined fire-hazard area, must certify that the property has passed a 'Defensible Space' state inspection.

Only 16 months ago. 'Grid broke' – see Texas Tribune online article dated 2/15/22; for 'snow too deep,' the average annual snowfall in the U.S. is 28" – for Dallas (Central TX) and Tyler (East TX, 90 min NW of Nacogdoches), the annual average is 1" while in Amarillo (in the TX panhandle) averages are more like 18".

Promise of rebound: March 2022. Nacogdoches, designated in 2013 by the Texas state legislature as the 'Garden Capital of Texas,' is famous for its azaleas (the 'pinks and plums' in the poem). The Ruby M. Mize Azalea Garden, the largest azalea garden in Texas, is situated on eight forested acres along LaNana Creek, on the campus of Stephen F. Austin State University. (For more on the natural sights and sounds along the LaNana Creek Trail, see my *LaNana Creek Haiku*, 2014, Xlibris.)

Fond hopes of spring. Snapdragons (genus *Antirrhinum*) are native to rocky areas of Europe, Africa, the U.S., and Canada. In Russia, edible oils are extracted from the seeds; leaves and flowers, considered to have anti-inflammatory properties, have been used for poultices to put on wounds; and a green dye can be made from the flowers.

Long hot summer. Cicadas are members of the insect order Hemiptera, and are found around the world. They have 'emergence' cycles that vary from one to thirteen or seventeen years; the latter type, called 'periodicals' occur only in North America. They make their loud sounds by using 'tymbals,' corrugated exoskeletal paired structures located on either side of the abdomen, which are vibrated rapidly by special muscles, creating a sound that be as loud as 106 dB SPL (conversational speech is 60-70 dB SPL, and a jet plane flyover at 1000 feet is around 130; sounds above 85 dB SPL can damage human hearing). Some moths also have tymbals, with slightly different structure and placement; their sounds are rarely audible to humans, but may be used to jam bat sonar as a means of protection against predation.

Weeks and weeks over 100. In Tyler TX (just NW of Nacogdoches), the *average* annual number of days at or above 100 degrees is seven; in 2022, between June 12 and August 16, Tyler recorded 44 such days; and as of July 31, San Antonio – 200 miles W of us, along the eastern border of the Hill Country – had counted 50 days over 100. The dove mentioned in the poem is the mourning dove (*Zenaida macroura*). The reference to mockingbirds (*Mimus polyglottos*) that 'don't sing' – although presented in the poem as though they went silent because of the heat – actually describes a glimpse of 'normality,' given the fact that the period between late August and late September is the usual 'time-out' when mockingbirds, who have two breeding seasons per year (Feb-Aug and Sept-Nov), stop singing.

Gerbera maintenance schedule. Gerberas are members of the Asteraceae family, with more than 20 recognized species. They are native to areas of tropical Africa, from which they have been introduced around the world as cultivars (garden flowers, usually a cross of two south-African forms, *Gerbera jamesonii* and *G. vindifolia*, known as *Gerbera x hybrida*). According to Wikipedia, they are the fifth most popular cut flower. They are also known as African daisies, Transvaal daisies, and Veldt daisies. The genus is named in honor of the 18th century German botanist Traugott Gerber, a medical doctor and a friend of Carl Linnaeus, the Swedish botanist who designed the system we use today for naming organisms. Pollinators such as bees, butterflies, and birds are attracted to Gerberas, but deer avoid them because of their coumarin-based bitter taste.

Pond at the bottom of our hill. The geological history of East Texas includes several cycles of sea incursions, which have in the past reached well up into North America. Current surface geology around Nacogdoches still reveals this history, along with evidence of post-ocean erosion patterns leaving ridges of younger rocks, while cutting down to reveal strata of older ones. Three such ridges, trending north to south, frame the city of Nacogdoches, all topped by the Sparta Sand Formation (our house sits on Sparta Sand), a formation which in some places is saturated with freshwater down to 120 feet. The city sits on the middle ridge of the three, and is separated from the ridge to the west by Banita Creek, and from the ridge to the east by LaNana Creek. There are springs throughout East Texas, including the two that form the headwaters of Banita and LaNana Creeks, both of which rise north of Nacogdoches, and flow south of town to drain into the 120-mile-long Angelina River, known for its populations of alligators.

Escape of the velvet ant. The velvet 'ant' (*Dasymutilla occidentalis*) is actually a solitary (not social) wasp in the same order (Hymenoptera) as ants and bees. The wingless females look like large, furry ants (up to an inch long), and can run very fast; the males have wings, which make them look more like wasps. I have seen only two velvet ants in my life, one in northern New Mexico, and the second in Nacogdoches, during the summer of 2022. I had my camera ready as I followed along after the scurrying female, but she didn't stop long enough for me to get a good shot. (I was fortunate to find an excellent online photo, taken by Mark Musselman, USFWS, available as public domain under the Creative Commons Free Use license.) The last line of the poem is based on the Citizens Band (CB) radio phrase 'Eastbound and down' often used by truckers, and quoted in the song of the same name sung by Jerry Reed, who co-wrote it with Deena Kaye Rose for the 1977 film *Smokey and the Bandit*. The phrase means, 'I'm driving East, and am leaving my CB channel open to continue the conversation.'

Succulents are right at home. The jokes here are all in reference to the fact that tequila is made from these striking plants, the Weber blue agave (*Agave tequilana*), a type of succulent (*not* a 'cactus') which is cultivated for making tequila, primarily in the Mexican state of Jalisco. When a plant matures (six to ten years), the leaves are cut away, the core (called a piña – it looks like a pineapple or pine cone) is baked and then shredded to extract the juice, which is then fermented, distilled, and aged. One mature plant can yield enough juice for 10-11 bottles of tequila. (Other related drinks, such as pulque and mezcal, are made from different agaves – there are more than 300 agave species.) *Patrón* is a brand of blue-agave tequila, and the phrase *'El patron,'* meaning 'the boss,' is intended both as a pun on the brand name and a gesture of respect to the toughness of this dramatic succulent. Tequila is typically drunk by first taking a lick of salt, then drinking, then biting a wedge of lime, thus the final joke about the 'spiny teeth' that line the edges of the leaves, which can reach seven feet long.

Cattle egrets' roosting tree. *Bubulcus ibis* is native to Africa, but appeared in South America in the late 1800s (no source I've found seems to know how they got there). They follow large grazing animals, to feed on invertebrates, including insects like grasshoppers, stirred up by the grazers' walking and eating. Local common names in the many places they occur often cite the animals they associate with in this way – rhinoceros egrets, cow birds, cow herons, elephant herons, etc. They are a small type of heron (family Ardeidae), about 20 inches high, with a three-foot wingspan. They often pass the night roosting in trees, leaving shortly after sunrise to spend the day foraging in fields with grazers, and returning to their home tree an hour before sunset.

Designated look-outs. During the day, cattle egrets don't spend all their time walking after grazers; they can often be seen standing in fields alone or in groups, as shown in the photo, and may occasionally stand on the back of a resting grazer, where they find other insects such as ticks, and may also 'keep a look-out' for additional grazers, as suggested in the poem.

Impersonating roseates. My husband and I first learned about cattle egrets when we lived in Oklahoma, and were delighted to find them again in the fields around Nacogdoches. In the summer of 2022, our house happened to be located on a local flyway which one flock used to get from their roosting tree to certain nearby cattle farms. (I don't know if 'local flyway' is an actual ornithological term, but I'm using it to refer to the regular route the birds took, analogous to the long-distance flyways of seasonal migrations that can span tens of thousands of miles.) On one of my early-morning walks (avoiding the daunting heat of afternoon), I saw a small group as described in the poem, flying in a V-formation against blue sky, high enough for their underwings to catch the pink light of the rising sun.

Our time spent at birding centers along the Texas Gulf Coast have made me fond of roseate spoonbills, who are the same pink I saw that morning on the cattle egrets. The vision provided me with the poem, but sadly, no actual photo, as I was too slow in unpacking my camera before the birds were out of sight. Thus the picture accompanying the poem substitutes small white clouds for the small white birds, but I was careful to take it at the same hour of day that I saw the birds, with sunrise just beginning to color the pines.

Finally, rain. The heat wave finally broke, with rains that arrived the week of August 19, 2022. Still, they were not enough to end the drought that Texas had been suffering since the previous fall. As of late summer 2022, 97% of the state population was still living under 'abnormally dry to exceptional' drought conditions. More than 400 water systems across the state had imposed water restrictions, and some areas had to have water shipped in. Across the state, July was the fifth driest, and the second warmest, ever recorded, and reservoirs were at least 20% below normal levels. Though not as severe as the 2011-12 Texas drought, the situation was still extremely serious, with forecasters predicting things would not improve until December, if then.

Puffball (?) mushroom. When I first saw this mushroom, the day after our rain break, it was a large white ball sitting flat on the ground as shown, with no visible stalk. Searching online, I tentatively identified it as a puffball. In two days, the stalk appeared, lifting the head about two inches above the ground, and allowing me to peek underneath to find it had gills. I have not been able to identify the type, though it seems to fit the specifications of *Agaricus bisporus*, 'common mushroom,' sometimes marketed as 'portobello.'

Fungi everywhere. This mushroom was pale yellow when I first saw it, in a flower pot along the curb of a neighbor's yard, the morning following a rain. When I lightly touched it to feel the texture, it was so fragile ('tender as a petal' says the poem) in its connection to the soil in the pot, one of the structures fell back flat. Though I returned hoping to see more arrive, within two days the delicate growths had disappeared. The web suggested these were examples of the Yellow Houseplant Fungus (*Leucocoprinus birnbaumii*), commonly seen in pots with nutrient-rich soil.

Snail after rain. One morning, again after a light rain, as I was washing dishes at our kitchen sink, I looked up and saw this snail moving across the screen right at my (and her) eye-level. I grabbed my camera and took photos from the inside, and then went outside, where I snapped this picture. I believe this is an Asian trampsnail (*Bradybaena similaris*), native to Southeast Asia and invasive to East Texas. The Wikipedia page attributes its common name to its fondness for locating on freight containers, which has apparently resulted in its rapid spread around the world.

September resurgence. We were astounded at the rebound following the rains' arrival, the burgeoning riot of green, and bushes full of blossoms, that sprang up on all sides as though it were March again. In the refreshingly cool days that followed, the amazing transformation reminded us why we love this part of Texas. The photo shows a bloom on an 'August beauty' gardenia bush (*Gardenia jasminoides*) along the front of our house, with some river rocks below. When I was growing up in Austin TX, my maternal grandmother planted several gardenia bushes around our house-on-a-hill, and my mother routinely wore a fresh gardenia blossom when she dressed for church on Sunday. The rich odor of gardenias always takes me back to those peaceful days, and these flowers were the first I planted around our house in Nacogdoches more than 20 years ago in 2001, the spring we moved to Texas.

Rainy sunset. After our visits to the Texas Gulf Coast, I've come to call this type of cloud formation 'coastal clouds' – because they remind me of the dramatic 'cloud-shows' that come and go on a regular basis along the coast, an ongoing entertainment that changes from hour to hour and day to day. During our heat wave in Nacogdoches, scarcely a cloud was in the sky from morning to night, but with the rains' return, it was reassuring to see the 'coastal messengers' back again, with their promise of ocean-sky theatrics, and water-on-the-way.

Deck-the-halls fall. Sprays of Virginia creeper (*Parthenocissus quinquefolia*), also called 'five-leaved ivy,' adorn the pine fences around our yard, and we look forward to the time of year when the deep forest-green of their chestnut-tree-like green palmate leaves transform into bright poinsettia-red. East Texas has its occasional years of subtle color changes in the deciduous trees scattered around the lush, rolling acres of pineywoods, but the creepers can be counted on to reveal their hidden anthocyanin (red) pigment in a burst of color just when we need it most, heralding a cool rainy fall and a mild green winter to come.

Hurricane season dead ahead [photo and poem follow the notes]. Hurricanes have a series of 'spiral rain-bands' (also called 'outer bands') extending out from the eye, which rotate together horizontally around the center of the storm. Because these bands of thunderstorms can contain winds as strong as a hurricane or a tropical storm, damage from an overall hurricane event can result from the paradoxical situation of outer-band winds moving *in different directions* from the main path of the storm (i.e., as the main storm moves onshore, band winds may be blowing in an offshore direction; north-to-south vs. the storm's opposite; east-to-west instead of west-to-east, etc.). The width of these bands varies, but can be in the hundreds of miles – for example, when Hurricane Gilbert, the second strongest tropical cyclone on record for the Caribbean, made landfall in September 1988 on the Yucatan Peninsula as a Category 5 storm, the set of outer bands reached 500 miles out from the eye. The 'meso' music in the poem refers to mesocyclones, air masses that begin moving in response to wind shear, and begin rising then circulating (rotating) around a vertical axis; they can occur within thunderstorms, and may go on to form tornados, something that can also happen within the strong thunderstorms inside hurricane rain-bands.

As for the wind outlook in East Texas, weather experts are saying that the country's 'tornado alley' is shifting away from its traditional locations, toward the south and east, targeting among other places, eastern Texas and Oklahoma. In April 2019 an F3 tornado ravaged the small town of Alto TX only 30 miles west of Nacogdoches, and last year another F3 crossed a highway only a few miles north. As recently as March of this year, a cluster of seven tornados touched down in East Texas, three of them F3s, and four F2s.

We have also learned to expect more intense hurricanes – since arriving in Nacogdoches in 2001, 200 miles from the Gulf Coast, we've witnessed the local effects of Hurricane Rita (September 2005, Category 3 at landfall), Ike (September 2008, Category 2) and more recently, Harvey (late August 2017, Category 4), all of which caused devastation not only along the coast but also across large areas of south and east Texas. Often the coastal damage was very close to

62

where we spend a month each winter, near Mustang Island and Port Aransas, and we observed the results later in the year – another reason we were glad we had the Generac.

Both of us previously lived in 'tornado alleys,' but never in the path of hurricanes, and we quickly learned the concept of 'outer bands,' and to respect their power. We saw what outer-band winds could do on the coast itself (land-to-ocean airflows so strong they created 'reverse-direction' wave-fronts that buckled large concrete sidewalks, and plowed through our favorite Port-Aransas birding center, completely flattening the eight-foot-tall grasses of its thick surrounding marshland, and erasing the long curving boardwalk and two-story viewing tower). And we also witnessed first-hand how strong such winds could be even 200 miles from shore – whole trees blown down all over town, large broken branches thrown about, tall pines twisted back and forth by wind gusts as though shaken by a giant hand.

What comes next . . .

Hurricane season dead ahead

Still too close to the coast, here
where winds hum meso
music, clouds practice side-bands.

About the Author

Judith Lauter (JudithLauter.com) was born in Austin, Texas. When she was nine, her family moved to Michigan where she later met her husband, the poet Ken Lauter, in a poetry-writing seminar at the University of Michigan taught by Donald Hall (US Poet Laureate, 2006-7). The couple has subsequently lived in the deserts of Arizona, the mountains of Colorado, the prairies of Missouri and Oklahoma, and now make their home in the pineywoods of Nacogdoches TX.

Judith holds a BA in English literature, three master's degrees (creative writing, library/information science, and linguistics), and a PhD in communication sciences (Washington University in St. Louis). She taught and directed human neuroscience laboratories at major universities for more than three decades, before retiring in 2012 and returning to her first loves, photography and poetry.

In addition to scientific articles, chapters, and books (including *How is Your Brain Like a Zebra?* Xlibris, 2008, ZebraBrain.net), she has published poems in journals, most recently the *Wallace Stevens Journal* and *Interdisciplinary Studies in Literature and Environment*; and won two Hopwood Awards for poetry (University of Michigan), an Academy of American Poets prize (University of Denver), and the Norma Lowry Memorial Prize (Washington University). Her prize-winning photography has been compared to Eliot Porter's; reproductions (including selections from this book) are available at FineArtAmerica.com. She has published nine previous books of poetry-and-images with Xlibris, plus a book of photos and poems about Wallace Stevens, with the Stephen F. Austin State University Press (see next page for titles).

Other books of poetry and images by Judith Lauter

Year of Haiku. Xlibris, 2013

Light from the Left: Poems on paintings by Rembrandt. Xlibris, 2013

Sonora Spring Haiku. Xlibris, 2013

Pineywoods Summer Haiku. Xlibris, 2014

Rockies Autumn Haiku. Xlibris, 2014

Coastal Bend Winter Haiku. Xlibris, 2014

LaNana Creek Haiku. Xlibris, 2014

Lady Slipper Trail Haiku. Xlibris, 2016

Konza Tallgrass Prairie Haiku. Xlibris, 2017

The Poet in the Park; Wallace Stevens and Elizabeth Park. SFA Press, 2017

*Green is Certain; An autobiography with selected poems,
Volumes I (1944-1962) and II (1962-1966).* Xlibris, 2021

*Perturbations; An autobiography with selected poems,
Tucson & Denver (1966-1971).* Xlibris, 2022

———————————————

Reproductions of Dr. Lauter's photographs
are available as prints, greeting cards, etc.
at FineArtAmerica.com.

Printed in the United States
by Baker & Taylor Publisher Services